SELF-Inquiry
for Internal Bliss

Yogi Shanti Desai

Copyright © 2024 Yogi Shanti Desai
All rights reserved
www.yogishantidesai.com

Table of Contents

Gratitude……………………………………………i
Foreword……………………………………………1
Author's Remarks…………………………………..3
Chapter 1) Self-Inquiry..…………………………….9
Chapter 2) Vedanta……………………………..…33
Chapter 3) Vipashyana…………………..….……..47
Chapter 4) Practices for Self-Inquiry……….……..57
Chapter 5) Simplified Guidance…………………..69
About the Author………………………...………..97

Gratitude

Special thanks go to Gudjon Bergmann for his unwavering and long-term support in the formatting, editing, and in all other aspects of the book and book cover production, to Gene Fortunato for his help in organizing the principle ideas of the book, and to Suchita Rao for her impeccable sense of color and style of the book cover design.

Foreword

Yogi Shanti Desai has written a brilliant exposition on the eternal. His new book, Eternal Bliss, is a complete introduction for access into the eternal. For both beginner and advanced readers, it provides the methods and practices of self-inquiry, it provides a brief, historical reference to past wisdom, and it provides practical help to the reader with two meditations that prepare and open the mind to journey deeper into the self.

The book reminds us that eternal bliss and happiness are our basic nature. It reminds us that all we need to do is remove the layers, the veils, the identities, the obstacles that cover our true nature. Yogi Shanti Desai discusses the obstacles that present themselves today in our society: distraction caused by the fast pace of technology, anger, greed, and cultural and racial identity.

Yogi Shanti Desai was born in Gujarat State of India and migrated to the United States at a young age with his brother to study chemistry at Drexel University and teach yoga. After earning enough money to retire, he moved with his family to Ocean City, New Jersey, to teach yoga full-time. In Ocean City, he opened the Yoga Institute, where he held yoga classes and seminars. He was the founder of an ashram in Glassboro, New Jersey, and he was the owner of Prasad, a holistic restaurant and vitamin store in Ocean City, New Jersey. Yogi Shanti Desai is an international speaker and author of numerous books on yoga, meditation, and spirituality. The combination of his worldly life and his spiritual life makes his teachings a unique and relevant resource for today's readers and spiritual practitioners.

Gene Fortunato
Ocean City, NJ

Author's Remarks

I have been learning and teaching yoga for over 50 years. This book is the essence of wisdom I attained through my subjective study, analytical thinking, introspection, practice and experience. This book is a summary of tools needed for self-inquiry to know thyself.

The essence of my teachings:

- Learn the techniques of mindfulness and apply them in daily life.
- Accept and love yourself. Be on the right path towards the goal and enjoy living in the present. Be flexible and modify the means as necessary.
- Be rooted within and be alone. Stand on your own two feet.
- Be open and receptive. Do not follow anyone blindly. Study the original teachings subjectively.
- Recognize that you are the co-creator of your experiences.

- Stop looking outside. Stop looking for the answers in the past or future. Settle down, be quiet and find peace within yourself.
- Become empty to receive. Purify and sharpen your intellect and use it to experience reality. Experience the changing nature of Jagat as Maya.
- Affirm and retain your true identity as an undercurrent, as an observer or witness.
- Follow the Vedanta chart for reference and guidance for introspection.

This book:

- Explains the meaning and purpose of self-inquiry and its urgent need today.
- Describes the chronological history of masters of self-inquiry.
- Provides a simple technique of awareness of breath with variation and application.
- Gives direction and guidance to wake-up seekers.
- Provides inspirational thoughts for introspection.

Main Points on Eternal Bliss and Self-inquiry

1. Eternal Bliss

Eternal bliss is our basic nature. We do not need to earn it; we only need to realize it by being still and focusing within. Everyone wants freedom from suffering and lasting peace, and people go in the wrong direction, seeking wealth, power, and fame to achieve it. They go in the wrong direction and are in illusion. This illusion is created by avidya or ignorance, where ignorance means not knowing our own nature. It is bombarded by constant conditioning of religions, society, inner desires and temptations.

2. Personal Duty (dharma)

We are born with natural duties. Duties to our family, society, and salvation come from performing our duty properly. It is called swadharma. Personal duty performed with love and attachment gives liberation. Our personal duty, seen perhaps as inferior to the duties imposed by society, when performed properly, gives us a greater liberation than trying to perform a superior or another person's duty. All the rituals and austerities are not necessary. Personal duties are usually prescribed by spiritual masters and religions, but one's ultimate personal duty is given by intuition. You can sacrifice all the other authorities when you awaken intuition.

3. We Are All Connected

The entire universe is made up of earth, water, fire, air, and space. It changes form but is never destroyed. All inert things like mountains, oceans, rivers, animals, insects, and all living creatures are connected with each other. If we realize this, the world would be a beautiful place. Our thoughts, speech, and actions are also interconnected. Thought is the most powerful starting point that influences speech and action. They collectively influence human beings, animals, and environments and can transform society. All the experiments show that thoughts can change the material world and heal insects, animals, and the world. Loving all living creatures will give peace in the world. Yet, we are alone from birth to death. We are alone when we are sleeping, eating, experiencing pleasure and pain. We are alone at death. We have to establish a connection with ourselves and attain friendship with ourselves.

4. Selfless Service

Selfless service is produced with love without expectation of any reward. It brings success, peace and freedom. To find happiness, one should invent selfless service that they can produce in their daily life.

5. Nothing is Permanent.

We are not the doer or enjoyer or sufferer. We are only the observer and witness. Pleasure and pain do not touch us. We are always blissful consciousness. Birth and death are an illusion. Pleasure and pain are illusions. They are like a wheel; they rotate constantly. Our consciousness, our permanent self, Atman, is not touched by them.

6. Charity Begins at Home

Charity begins at home; you do not need to go elsewhere. Build your health, energy, money, time, wisdom, and compassion so it is available at any time. If you lack them, you become a burden. Your presence becomes a source of love and peace.

7. Practice Aloneness

Practicing aloneness means observing silence and abstaining from harmful thoughts, speech, and actions. Prevent activities that build attachment to the world, material objects, and emotions. Worldly or material activities and desires build attachments and stress. Practicing aloneness revives energy, builds intuition, and makes you a master to guide others, an instrument of inspiration.

8. Kali-Yuga

We are in Kali-Yuga now, the dark age of spirituality with speed. The yuga cycles are similar to the cycles of nature; they are like day and night, the rising and falling of tides, the seasons—they change constantly. We are approaching Satya yuga, the spiritual spark. Utilize the speed in Kali-Yuga for your personal spiritual evolution.

Chapter 1) Self-Inquiry

Self is our innermost eternal essence. It is the subject of the projected impermanent world. Realizing the Self is the ultimate attainment of liberation. Searching for the Self is the essence of life. Self is with us at all times. People in ignorance search for peace and happiness in the world, whereas wise people look within.

We are born in the human body and mind and identify with it. We are programmed from birth as being male/female and having a name, race, and religion. We start accepting these as limitations and forget that our nature is pure consciousness without boundaries.

Self-inquiry includes the study of Atman (the Sanskrit name of the Self) and all the faculties it utilizes to function in the world. Atman, covered with layers of ignorance or an ever-changing world (known as Maya in Sanskrit), is called Jivatma (the Sanskrit equivalent to the Western soul). Bound to duality, Jivatma forgets its own perfect nature and looks for happiness in the world.

The concepts of Atman and Jivatma are very old. Atman is the Self, and Jivatman is the breathing Self or live being. Two birds are perched in a tree. One bird is eating the fruit of the tree, and the other is watching. The bird that is eating the fruit is Jivatma, and the bird that is watching is Atman. The tree is the body.

Antahkaran is the Sanskrit name for Jivatma's total personality. Collectively, all human faculties, including body, senses, mind, intellect and unconscious mind, are Antahkaran. One has to understand the functions of all these faculties to master them. Antahkaran literally means inner (antah) instrument (karan) or inner sense organ, inner-cause. It is the totality of the mind: the manas (mind), buddhi (intellect), chitta (memory or consciousness), ahamkara (I-ego). The extent to which you inquire into antahkaran is the extent to which your experience and knowing will be profound.

The goal of life is to remove all veils of ignorance and to know our true essence. If you want to master the Self, you have to get to know the mind, intellect and unconscious mind. That is the beginning of self-inquiry.

Freedom or Bondage?

Jivatma can choose the direction of either freedom or bondage.

Bondage: Jivatma becomes deluded by Antahkaran, and chooses the path of pleasure (Preya), and gets tangled in the world. Jivatma becomes extroverted with the identity of MINE and OURS. MINE refers to possessions, fame, power and loved ones. OURS refers to illusory identity with race, religion, nationality, culture, and political party. Jivatma, in bondage, tries to find an escape in the activities and glamour of life. People in bondage become short-sighted, seek relief from suffering, and forget to search for it during pleasures. They do not wake up from duality and repeat the cycle of transmigration, a continuation from life to life due to unfulfilled desires until sanskaras (deep unconscious impressions) are exhausted.

Freedom: To attain freedom, you allow Jivatma to purify Antahkaran, see reality, choose the path of virtue (Sreya) and follow the spiritual path to liberation. Attractions to wealth, pleasure, power and fame do not tempt. You become a visionary, face reality and look within for answers. You are not tempted by impulses, realize that the world is filled with suffering from birth until death, learn to flow with life, accept the relative reality of the material world and live fully without attachments. Once you create a surplus, you remain content and aware of ultimate reality as a constant undercurrent and use world reality as a means. You accept the impermanent world as if it were a dream. By using mindfulness, awareness and wisdom, you will find guidance for your life.

Awaken to Your True Nature

People are programmed to accept themselves as just the physical body. They search for temporary pleasure from the sense organs and forget that their needs for survival and pleasure make them slaves and dependent. Yet, this is not true. We are lions and have become like sheep living in the company of sheep. True masters can awaken you to explore your true nature, which is not limited by body, senses and mind. Your existence in human form is relatively short, while your true nature is eternal.

The Essence of Self-Inquiry

- All the masters recommended a moral life (Dharma) as a personal foundation. They recommended mastery of senses and the mind and to go within and "Know Thyself." They recommended restricting extroverted activities and performing duties selflessly without attachments.
- Peace comes in proportion to introversion, and bondage comes in proportion to extroversion.
- The goal of life is to end suffering and find lasting peace.
- We need to become free from transmigration (the birth and death cycle).

- Self is our essential nature. It is an eternal consciousness of bliss. It is covered with layers of illusions (Maya). Wake up, remove the veils of Maya and experience bliss.

The Vedanta chart on page thirty-two explains the direction for liberation.

The Need for Self-Inquiry in Today's Society

Currently, we are at the end cycle of the four yugas. Each yuga cycle is comprised of thousands of years of creation, sustenance and transformation, similar to the cyclical changes of day/night and changing seasons.

We are currently passing through Kali-Yuga, which represents darkness, ignorance, and spiritual blindness. Kali-Yuga cannot be avoided. It is the dark age of spirituality, where people are lost in ignorance and immorality at the same time. In Satya-Yuga, Lord Krishna declared that out of thousands of people, perhaps one is searching for the higher Self. In the current age of Kali-Yuga, the percentage is even smaller because there are more distractions. The short video clip was once defined to be 5 minutes on YouTube, but now the short video clip is 30 seconds on TikTok. In Kali-Yuga, one who wakes up can evolve faster because speed is a central feature of this period. Utilize this speed with awareness to learn lessons quicker and go in the right direction. In Kali-Yuga, the speed of things will take precedence and present opportunities for sincere seekers.

Characteristics of Kali-Yuga

Immorality and Corruption

Dharma (morality) is the foundation for the health and peace of individuals and society. Currently, Adharma (immorality) pervades humanity. We are surrounded by immorality at home, in business and in society. Immorality produces stress due to insecurity. One is preoccupied with self-defense and survival. Here are some examples: Businesses encourage impulsive quick fixes instead of individuals taking personal responsibilities. Smoking and narcotic drugs are killing new generations, yet no progress has been made in prevention. Mass murders are becoming commonplace, and no progress is being made to control firearms. The young generation is suffering from depression and mental sickness. The global environment is polluted regularly and ignored by short-sighted leaders. Fast food chains are ruining our health and are spreading globally to poorer nations.

Population Explosion

The world's population is increasing at an alarming rate. It was 1 billion in 1800, 8 billion currently, and it is projected to be 10 billion in 2053. The population explosion will cause food shortages, water shortages, starvation and climate change. An increased population will consequently drive up environmental pollution as further demands are put on the planet.

Speed and Changes

Things are changing at an exponential rate. Technology is advancing rapidly, and normal tools are becoming obsolete. We have become dependent on gadgets and have lost the capacity to enjoy a simple life. Gadgets are controlling the lives of all family members who have lost the capacity for communication. There are more tools for comfort and luxury, yet people complain about the lack of happiness, money and time.

Divided Society

There is a lack of unity in society. There is discrimination of race, color, wealth and education. Political parties look out for their own gain instead of serving society as a whole.

Loads of Information

Bombardment of information hypnotizes us. We have lost the capacity to think and be creative. As the mind expands with information, our heart sinks and loses the capacity for love and compassion. The new generation has become smarter but lacks wisdom.

Suffering from Avidya (Ignorance)

True knowledge provides peace and contentment under all circumstances. In Kali-Yuga, people suffer from Avidya (seeing the impermanent as permanent, suffering as pleasure, impure as pure, etc.). They cannot see the true nature of things. They have become short-sighted and impulsive instead of being aware and wise. They are attracted to a changing world and are victims of duality. They are controlled by cycles of pleasure/pain, gain/loss and success/failure. People do not have the vision to see that pleasure produces cravings for future pleasures and leaves Sanskaras (deep subconscious imprints) that produce slavery in the mind. They seek happiness from objects that have no capacity to provide happiness. Happiness is perceived by a quiet mind. Everything changes constantly, including the material world, mind and emotions. In order to remain free, people should be at their center and observe changing thoughts. People are programmed to believe in some religion. They get attached to a belief system and get bombarded by authorities who rely on dogma and the writings of others. They get established in blind faith and get offended when challenged. They defend their beliefs blindly. This is a self-created illusion.

Cultivating Vidya (Wisdom):

Vidya is true wisdom that directs life and leads one to freedom from suffering. Each of us has a choice to maintain our inner stillness and survive the influence of Kali-Yuga. People who remain at their center are not touched by the turmoil of the world. The center of a storm remains still.

To obtain freedom from ignorance:

1. Focus on the inner permanent Self and impermanent nature of the world. Remain as a passive witness to a changing world.
2. Use the techniques of observing and harmonizing breath.
3. Practice mindfulness while doing activities.
4. Cultivate awareness to learn lessons from the experiences of your life.
5. Expand your consciousness and cultivate unconditional love.
6. Remove attachments to things and people. You will grow with wisdom as you age.
7. Remain in the present instead of the past or future. Quiet your mind and become connected to the Self.

Vidya removes suffering. Vidya provides the light that removes the darkness of ignorance. Purified Antahakaran provides the path of Sreya (virtue) and Dharma (morality) to end suffering.

We Are All Interconnected (Selfless Service)

The only way we can find bliss is by making others happy. You don't have to do lots of meditation or austerities. You only need to perform your swardharma (personal duty). Personal duty is a duty to family, work, society, nature, and all living creatures. The ego and the mind are the cause of all suffering. To remove this suffering, practice selfless service.

The History and Evolution of Self-Inquiry

The ancient Indus Valley Civilization was developed some 4,500 years ago. This was where the foundation of spiritual exploration was built. Ancient seers (rishis) in India experienced many spiritual truths. This direct experience is called Darshana. Their teachings were classified into the six classical philosophies (Shad Darshans) of India. Of the six philosophies, the three major Darshans are (1) Sankhya, (2) Vedanta, and (3) Yoga. Sankhya and Vedanta are philosophies that teach the direction to discover the Self. Yoga provides the techniques to accomplish Self-Realization.

You can derive inspiration and guidance from past masters by being open and receptive. Ideally, we should study their teachings in the original language and derive their teachings intuitively. Today, however, we are in a different time and place, and our needs are different as well. We have to adopt their teachings and utilize these for contemporary times and in a practical way. All the past masters were revolutionary, and their teachings were suitable for their time in history. In turn, their followers became dogmatic and turned the original teachings into uncompromising and literal religions. To go beyond dogma, we need to understand the essence of their teachings.

- Sankhya of Kapila (documented in 300 AD)
- Vedanta of Badarayan (500 BC-200 AD)
- Eightfold path of Patanjali (documented in 200 BC)
- Eightfold path of Buddha (563-480 BC)
- Non-dual Vedanta of Aadi Shankaracharya (788-820 AD)
- Self-Inquiry of Ramana Maharshi (1879-1950 AD)
- Quantum physics (1900 AD)
- Vipassana Practice of Goenka (1924-2013)
- Threefold Path (published 2018)

Sankhya Philosophy

Sankhya was written in 300 AD by Kapila. It explains creation in a scientific manner. The Universe is created by Consciousness merging with matter (union of Purusha and Prakriti) and the interaction of three qualities (Gunas) of nature. Sankhya explains the world as a macrocosm and all living creatures as a microcosm. The Universe is comprised of 24 elements, and the Self is the 25th element (transcendental). The 24 elements include the body, sense organs, motor organs, mind, intellect, chitta and I-consciousness. The goal is to rise above these elements, experience the Self and become free.

Vedanta Philosophy

Vedanta includes the Upanishads, Bhagavad Gita and the Brahma Sutras. These scriptures were written between 500 BC and 200 AD. Many Upanishads were written by unknown masters. The basic teaching is that Brahman is the eternal reality. It has no beginning or end. It is infinite (non-dual). With a limited mind, one perceives God as the three forces of nature (Gunas) or Gods of creation (Brahma), sustenance (Vishnu) and destruction (Mahesh).

Cosmic illusion (Maya) covers reality with its powers of concealment (avaran) and projection (vikshep). With concealing power, one gets lost in the wrong identity of one's own being. With projection power, one gets lost in the material universe. The goal is to wake up from the illusions of Maya, realize Atman (Brahman) and become free. Maya means magic, illusion, and appearance. It calls the seeker to discern between what is true and what is false.

Yoga

Philosophies and practices include Raja Yoga of Patanjali, which was compiled in 200 BC. He presented the total process of philosophies and practices, spiritual powers, and liberation in four small chapters of 195 Sutras (short condensed phrases) that carry essential messages. Many authorities recognize it as a basic source of wisdom and have written commentaries on it. Patanjali focused on Raja Yoga and did not provide details on Hatha Yoga, only telling practitioners to sit steadily.

Between 1300 and 1600 AD, textbooks on Hatha Yoga were written. These books provided details about yoga positions, breathing and kundalini practices.

Since 1960, yoga gained popularity, especially in the West. The essence of Yoga has now become diluted and has turned into simple exercise routines. Many leaders have formed sequences of yoga postures and have given brand names such as Iyengar yoga, Sivananda yoga, Bikram yoga, Power yoga, Hot yoga etc. People have become preoccupied with the means and have ignored the goal of Hatha Yoga. Hatha Yoga is a means for Raja Yoga and the ultimate attainment of liberation.

The Sankhya and Vedanta philosophies provide different approaches, whereas Yoga provides guidance for practical application. The Raja Yoga of Patanjali provides the eight-fold path to liberation.

1. Yama: Five restraints
2. Niyama: Five moral codes
3. Asana: Yoga positions
4. Pranayama: Breathing practice
5. Pratyahara: Sense withdrawal
6. Dharana: Concentration
7. Dhyana: Meditation
8. Samadhi: Absorption

Yama and Niyama form the fundamental ethical foundation of practice. One does not find peace until one learns to flow with life. Asana and Pranayama purify the body and nervous system. Pratyahara and Dharana gather and focus energy. Dhyana and Samadhi unveil Atman and cause liberation. The first four comprise Hatha Yoga, a practice that creates a foundation and prepares the body for the mental challenges of the last four steps of Raja Yoga.

Eightfold Path of Buddha

Lord Buddha (563-480 BC) was a revolutionary master. Originally, he was born into a Hindu family where he received ancient teachings. He then spent six years with yoga masters and went through severe austerities. Unsatisfied, he went on his own inner search, where he discovered the middle path. After reaching enlightenment, he spent 40 years teaching his disciples and sharing his knowledge. His eightfold path simplifies the Raja Yoga path.

Sheela (Moral behavior similar to Yama and Niyamas)
1. Right speech (Vacha)
2. Right conduct (Karma)
3. Right livelihood (Ajivika)

Samadhi (Deep concentration)
4. Right effort (Vyayam)
5. Right awareness (Smriti)
6. Right contemplation (Samadhi)

Pragnya (Wisdom)
7. Right contemplation (Sankalpa)
8. Right understanding (Drishti)

Through his search, Buddha found four noble truths: One, life is suffering (slightly out of place); two, cause; three, cure; and four, the eightfold path to remove suffering and attain Nirvana. Nirvana is defined as the extinction of ego and the removal of suffering. Conversely, Vedanta's goal is to remove suffering and attain eternal bliss. Since then, Buddhist authorities and Vedanta authorities have been in disagreement about how to find liberation. Buddha calls for Nirvana (shoonya or zero), while Vedanta calls for Brahman (infinity or source of bliss). Awakened persons will not find any conflicts between these two philosophies.*

*For further understanding, refer to my book, *Zero is Infinity*, published in 2015 and available through Amazon.

Buddha recommended three refuges for spiritual practice:

1. Dharma (moral living)
2. Buddha (Enlightened one).
3. Sanga (group of monks) or Satsang.

His path was for personal salvation and was called Hinyana (Lower Vehicle) or Theravada Buddhism. Its popularity spread throughout Southeast Asia. Four hundred years after Buddha's death, a monk from south India named Nagarjuna revolutionized Buddha's teachings. Nagarjuna's approach further called for the salvation of humanity. It was called Mahayana (Greater Vehicle) and spread throughout China and Japan. In China, it was adapted into

Chinese culture and became known as Chen. In Japan, it was adopted into Japanese culture and became known as Zen. Both Chen and Zen mean Dhyana or meditation. Around 500-600 AD, Buddhist teachings spread to Tibet and included tantra and rituals. This was called Vajrayana.

Buddha was interested in quick enlightenment instead of a lengthy process of exploration. Sincere people do not need to waste time and get lost in the means. Buddha's path is a direct path for sincere seekers. In his teachings, the Pali language replaced Sanskrit. Like Latin, Sanskrit was no longer used in everyday society.

Buddha's Simplified Teachings

Sheela: Buddha simplified the ten disciplines of Raja Yoga into three major disciplines. One does not need to waste time in following elaborate disciplines. Instead, one can focus on liberation. The three basic disciplines are the essence of the ten disciplines of Yama and Niyama.

Samadhi: Buddha eliminated yoga positions, breathing practices, and sense withdrawal and introduced right awareness (Samyak Smriti) to quieten the mind. In Pali, this is called Samyak Sati. At that time, life was very hard, and the process of survival provided the necessary exercises without additional time and effort. Buddha focused on preparing the mind for enlightenment. Today, postures, breathing practices, and sense withdrawal are useful tools for many practitioners but can be a waste of time for sincere seekers.

Pragnya: Buddha used the Vipassana technique to observe the impermanent nature of the body (kaya), sense perceptions (vedna), and memories (Chitta). In Raja yoga, Samadhi was developed in four stages until one reached seedless (Nirbij) samadhi. Buddha's focus was to perceive reality directly through Vipassana practice instead of mastering Samadhi.

Practice: There are two main components of Buddha's path. One is awareness of incoming and outgoing breath (Anapan Sati) to quieten the mind. Two is Vipassana to observe Sanskaras and evaporate them.

Buddha was a sincere seeker and avoided unnecessary details. His path is direct.

In comparison, Raja Yoga and Hatha Yoga provide the necessary preparation for the body through yoga positions and mastery of the mind through breathing techniques. In modern times, with a greater amount of stress in life, one should utilize Hatha Yoga with positions and breathing techniques as a means to help with Buddha's path.

Advaita Vedanta (Non-dual Vedanta)

Aadi Shankaracharya (788-820 AD) is considered the authority on non-dual Vedanta. Advaita Vedanta does not emphasize belief in God. Rather, its concept of a supreme being is similar to quantum physics. Shankaracharya wrote many books which are considered to be textbooks for sincere seekers, including commentaries on the basic scriptures. He recommended the removal of illusions covering the body. These illusions are OURS, MINE and ME. When illusions are dissolved, what remains is Atman (the Self). Atman is the ultimate reality, while the world of ours, mine and me, are cosmic illusions (Maya). One negates all illusions one at a time and then practices affirmation of I-Consciousness (Atman).

Self-Inquiry of Ramana Maharshi (1879-1950)

Ramana Maharshi was a modern master. He broke away from all dogmas and taught the path of Self-Inquiry. His path is a pathless path that does not require any direction other than sincere personal inquiry and experience. He maintained that the Self within is the source of everything. One needs to inquire, "Who am I?" with a quiet mind and go to the source to find the answer with direct perception. He remained in solitude and was discovered by seekers through a book written by Paul Brunton. World seekers visited him for guidance, and they were awakened by his silent presence. He spoke very little and taught mostly in silence. Many awakened masters have carried his message.

Quantum Physics

Max Planck is considered the father of quantum physics. Modern quantum physics has scientifically validated the concept of non-dual Vedanta. It declared the universe a united field of consciousness. The entire universe is in a constant state of flux. Everything and everyone is interconnected. Nothing is created or destroyed. Visible gross, liquid or gaseous forms are due to interactions of electromagnetic energy. The entire universe is an empty space.

Vipashyana Practice of Goenka

Satya Narayan Goenka (1924-2013) was born in Burma into a successful Hindu family. In his youth, he had a severe migraine problem. He got treatments abroad without any success. He studied Vipassana under a Burmese Guru, and his migraine problem was solved. With his Guru's permission, he started teaching Vipassana. Vipassana (Pali spelling) of Hinyana Buddhism was mostly lost after Buddha's departure. Goenka brought Vipashyana (Sanskrit spelling) to India and started offering 10-day retreats as a service. Because they were beneficial, the retreats became very popular and spread around the world. Many teachers offered retreats to groups, prisons and other institutions.

One reason why the program became successful was that attendants were committed to the entire duration of the program and did not leave. They took vows of Dharma (morality), were provided simple food, and were not allowed to experience any distractions such as music and phones. They had to remain silent and practice Anapan Sati at all times. The meaning of Anapan Sati in Sanskrit is Prana and Apana Smriti. It means awareness of incoming prana and outgoing apana without effort. Attendants found it to be very difficult for several days, but then their minds yielded to inner silence. They were training for Vipashyana of the body (kaya), sensations (vedna) and unconscious thoughts (Chitta).

Threefold Path (published in 2018)

As previously mentioned, we are going through Kali-Yuga or the dark age of spirituality. It is a period of declining morality and exponential changes. There are more distractions than ever before. People do not have the time, money, energy or enthusiasm to maintain patience and perseverance (Abhyas and Vairagya). Their mind is distracted constantly. My threefold path is designed for simplified teachings and is suitable for modern times. There is no need to study complex philosophies or undergo harsh austerities. It does not require any specific beliefs. The threefold path is applicable in daily life, removes suffering and provides permanent bliss. The threefold path includes:

1. Dharma

Dharma means following the rhythm of nature and flowing with life. Do unto others what others do unto you. Instead of following the Ten Commandments or the ten yamas and niyamas of Raja Yoga, Dharma involves understanding and applying moral disciplines dynamically rather than mechanically. Dharma is guided by intuition and changes with each situation.

2. Stillness of Mind

Stillness is obtained by the passive observation of breath. Slowing down the breath slows down prana and the mind. A quiet mind goes to its source, which is I-Consciousness—the passive observer of the entire world. It observes changing thoughts, emotions and memories without judging.

3. Awareness of Self and Impermanence

Duality: Become Drishta (Observer). Maintain awareness of the permanent Self (I-Consciousness) and impermanence of the world. The Self is the subject, and the world is the object. Observe the world like watching a movie on the screen; remain a blissful observer. To aid in the awareness of self, the drishtis (objects of a focused gaze) may be used in the asanas, meditation and sense withdrawal.

Nonduality: Become Sakshi (Witness, Atman). There is only one universal observer found within. When you look within in silence, you become a witness. There is no duality. Only universal reality remains. You become like space. Things happen in space, yet fire or flood do not touch it. Space is indivisible. Become like a mirror that reflects all objects as a witness.

Difference between duality and nonduality. Duality is living in the world while being conscious. In a nondual state, one stops functioning in the world because one merges with everything. For the purpose of today's world, duality is more practical.

Summary

Every path offers different approaches to the ultimate Self.

CHART #3 ATMAN-JAGAT-BRAHMAN

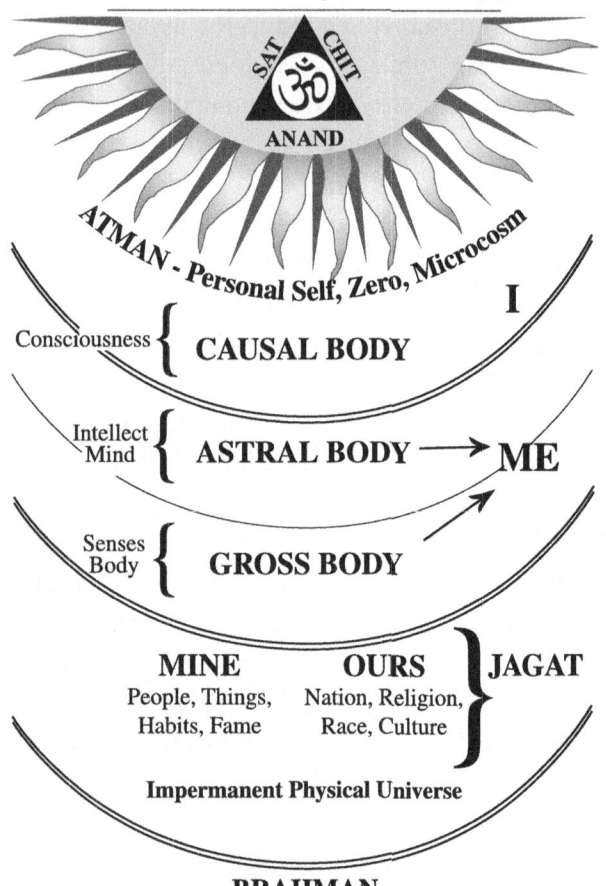

SAT CHIT ANAND

ATMAN - Personal Self, Zero, Microcosm

I

Consciousness { **CAUSAL BODY**

Intellect / Mind { **ASTRAL BODY** → **ME**

Senses / Body { **GROSS BODY**

MINE — People, Things, Habits, Fame

OURS — Nation, Religion, Race, Culture

} **JAGAT**

Impermanent Physical Universe

BRAHMAN
Universal Self, Infinity, Macrocosm

AUM Vibration

Chapter 2) Vedanta

Vedanta is an ancient philosophy that has been tried and applied for thousands of years. The following is a brief explanation of the Vedanta chart.

Atman/Brahman (drop/ocean) represent eternal consciousness whose nature is Sat (eternal existence), Chit (consciousness) and Anand (bliss). It is beyond time and space, beyond the past and future, and its power spreads to the causal body (I-Consciousness).

The causal body is subtlest and produces astral and gross bodies. The gross body is used while awake, the astral body during sleep, and the causal body in deep meditation. The causal body is like vapor, the astral body is like water, and the gross body is like an ice cube. The causal body is the most powerful and can influence our astral gross bodies. The causal body or I-consciousness is closest to Atman and is the subtlest choiceless observer of the material universe. Prana connects all the bodies.

I-Consciousness uses the mind, intellect, and chitta (unconscious mind) collectively. The combination of these four is called Antahkaran (Jivatma or soul). Jivatma is Atman in bondage due to the power of Maya (Avidya or ignorance). When Jivatma awakens and experiences its own nature, it becomes free.

Waking up Jivatma

To awaken awareness of Jivatma, one has to go inward, explore, rise above the material universe, and look within. This is done by removing wrong identities with a negation practice—such as the illusory burdens of OURS and MINERALS and identity with ME (body, senses, mind, intellect and chitta). When these identities are removed, one remains as I-Consciousness and affirms the qualities of Atman as Sat (eternal existence), Chitta (Consciousness) and Anand (Bliss).

Because of Maya, Jivatma identifies with the body, senses, mind and intellect. The practice of meditation removes coverings. Jivatma remains an observer and witness of mind, intellect and Chitta (Sanskrit for mind stuff). Purified Antahkaran is required for the experience of I-Consciousness.

When one transcends Jivatma and searches for the observer of I-Consciousness, only supreme consciousness (Atman) remains. Dualities disappear.

Personal identity disappears. One becomes universal consciousness. According to Vedanta, this is the goal of life. The experience ends all suffering and gives eternal bliss. It is considered liberation or freedom from transmigration (the cycle of repeated birth and death).

Experiences of the World

Everything in the world is impermanent and changing. Impermanent things cannot give lasting happiness. Furthermore, the mind is used as an instrument and changes constantly. It cannot give lasting happiness. All mental experiences are dualistic. Dualistic means pleasure and pain are the two sides of the same coin. The cycles of pleasure/pain, gain/loss, and success/failure revolve constantly. Only when one remains at the inner center and maintains equanimity will one transcend dualities and become free.

Jivatma, Jagat and Atman

Jivatma is in Jagat. You cannot run away from or escape it. Face bondage and use the experience as a means to become free from Jagat. Jagat is a relative reality—for the time being—while Atman is the eternal reality at all times. Jagat is a prison for Jivatma. The goal of life is to wake up from the dream of Maya (illusion) and realize your eternally blissful nature.

Faculties from the Outside to the Inside

Jagat is the material universe we live in. It includes all material objects and all living creatures. It constantly changes and is also called Sansar. Jagat is the cause of bondage or freedom. Jagat includes MINE and OURS.

MINE includes people, things, habits and fame. Things are material possessions such as homes, cars and boats. In reality, we have a belief in ownership and are possessed by them. Our fame, honors, power and degrees are only labels. They only have value if recognized by others. Honor or insult do not control us if we do not react to them. Our family relations are due to birth. We do not own them. They come into our lives to settle karmic debts. Attachments build due to association and expectation. Due to our attachments, we try to possess others and suffer. If we love our family without attachments, we find joy and freedom.

OURS means that we build identities with nationality, religion, race, culture or political party. Political parties, nationality and religion are only labels and can be changed. Labels give us an illusory identity, a feeling of belonging, and build our ego. This gives many an imaginary sense of superiority. A stronger identity means stronger bondage.

ME is made of the Gross body (Body and senses) and Astral body (Mind and intellect).

Atman identifying itself with coverings of Antahkaran— I + ME + Chitta (unconscious mind) — is called Jivatma (Soul).

Sharir (Body)

Annamaya Kosha: The body is made of five rudimentary elements (panch mahabhutas): earth, water, fire, air and space. It is called the food sheath because it is nourished by food and returns back to earth (the source). It changes constantly, ages, gets sick and dies. The body is called the field because it supports five sense organs, five motor organs, the nervous system, the mind and the intellect.

Prana (Sense Organs)

Pranamaya Kosha: Prana is subtler and is expressed as five sense organs and five motor organs. Five major pranas and five minor pranas regulate the functions of the entire body. Kundalini and seven chakras manage functions within the body. The entire body is made of prana. Prana pervades the entire body and the mind. Prana flows through astral nerve tubes called nadis.

Atman resides in the innermost center of the heart. It radiates prana through 101 major Nadis and

72,000 minor nadis. Prana enters the body at birth. Prana leaves the body at death. In a gross sense, prana is breath. The number of breaths determines our life span. One can lengthen life by maintaining the rhythm of breath. One can shorten life through stress, worries, anger and fear.

Manah (Mind)

Manaomaya Kosha: Manah is born when it pays attention to the passing thoughts. It perceives everything presented to it. It records everything without judging. Animals rely on the mind and follow their instinct. They do not hoard or worry about the future. Humans have intellect, and when they misuse it, they go against the laws of nature and suffer.

Buddhi (Intellect)

Vignanamaya Kosha: Intellect judges and chooses direction in life. Intellect is a gift to humans that animals do not have. It is the process of evolution. Intellect has a choice. It can choose the wrong direction in life and choose the path of pleasure (preya) and become worse than animals which choose the right direction due to innate instinct. If one chooses the path of virtue (shreya), he or she can find happiness and liberation.

We are programmed in life to react to each situation and choose an appropriate direction toward survival. Programming can also become habitual and generate compulsive actions that disturb our peace. Intellect is preoccupied with survival and worries about the future. It dwells in the pleasant memories of the past and tries to run away from unpleasant experiences.

Ahankar (I-Consciousness)

Anandmaya Kosha: Causal body It is the consciousness which is awareness of "I am." It has no past or future size or shape. It is used as Drishta (Observer) and Sakshi (Witness) to make you free. It can get tangled with the identity of body, senses, and mind and become Jivatma in bondage.

Chitta: (Unconscious mind) It is the total mind. It stores all the memories of past and past lives.
Chitta is a storehouse of memories. Bad memories create hindrances, and good memories support the personal path.

Chitta Vritti: Chitta manifests in the form of waves and disturbs inner tranquility. Yogi Patanjali defines yoga as mastering thought waves. There are five chitta vrittis. They exist at all times, whether in deep sleep or while awake, dreaming or thinking.

Chitta vrittis are:

1. Praman (Direct perception)
2. Viparyaya (Illusion)
3. Vikalpa (Delusion)
4. Nidra (Sleep)
5. Smriti (Memories)

The Raja Yoga path leads to mastery of the chitta vrittis.

Sanskara: All experiences of life leave impressions on the unconscious mind (Chitta).
There are deep sanskaras from childhood, mother's womb and previous lives. Sanskaras are stored in the subconscious and unconscious mind. The ultimate storage of sanskaras is in the body as five rudimentary elements (Punch mahabhootas). We are controlled by these sanskaras. These sanskaras can be removed from the body, senses and mind through Vipashyana meditation.

Swabhav: (Inner personality) Sanskaras become deeper with repetition and intensity. Shallow sanskaras are lines drawn in sand. Deep sanskaras are like carvings on the rock. Accumulated sanskaras of previous lives become our personality. Our swabhav becomes our undercurrent. It transcends logic. We are driven by it.

Antahkaran: Mind stuff or total mind. It is our total personality that includes synchronization of mind, intellect, chitta and Ahankar. It is our inner personality and measure of our spiritual evolution and wisdom. One uses wisdom to perceive reality as is. One cultivates spiritual discernment (Vivek) and renunciation (Vairagya) effortlessly. Ahankaran is pure consciousness. It is the invisible observer. It has no past or future. It does not judge or analyze. It remains a constant subject of all that is observed. All the objects of the world are impermanent and change constantly. One does not get attached, expect any reward, and ends up enjoying the present and flowing with life.

Atman/Brahman (Self): Atman is experienced in the innermost chamber of the spiritual heart. I-Consciousness is also experienced within the spiritual heart. Atman is universal and exists universally. Atman is reflected in all living creatures. It permeates animate and inanimate beings. It is omnipresent, omniscient and omnipotent.

Jivatma (Soul): Atman identifying itself with coverings of Antahkaran is called Jivatma (Soul) Antahkaran is I-consciousness using body, senses, mind, intellect and chitta (unconscious mind)

Atman Utilizes Body, Senses, Mind, Intellect and Chitta

The body is the field for the functions of all faculties. Sense organs are perceived by the mind. Motor organs follow the mind's command. The mind only hears information and records it. Intellect makes judgments. I-Conscious is the only subject of experience. I-Consciousness is the observer, and Atman is the witness. When I-Consciousness identifies with objects of experience, it gets enmeshed in Maya (cosmic illusion). One interprets experiences as pleasant or unpleasant and craves to repeat them. All the impressions are stored in the unconscious mind (Chitta) as memories. These memories and desires compel one to rebirth. This transmigration is considered bondage.

Intuition: When the mind becomes quiet and receptive, the light of Atman reflects in the mind and is recognized by I-Consciousness. This is called intuition. The voice of intuition is subtle. One needs to trust it. The climax of logic produces a transcendental state of no mind, leading to intuition. Intuition transcends time and space. It provides a panoramic view of life. It is visionary and free from impulsive thoughts and worries.

Mindfulness: Mindfulness is the practice of living in the present. One perceives things as they are. One does not use intellect to judge. Generally, one has the built-in response of like or dislike, judgment, and comparison. These drain lots of energy. One misses experiences in life. One observes the breath, slows it down and makes it rhythmic to experience objectively. One breaks down the activities into small steps and becomes a master of actions instead of being mechanical. One acts constructively instead of acting impulsively. One can apply mindfulness to actions such as walking, eating, talking or driving. Life becomes meditative. One acts constructively instead of reacting. One finds greater joy in simple acts of daily life. People who are not mindful do not enjoy what they have and waste energy on an illusory past and future.

Awareness: Mindfulness practice can lead one to awareness. Awareness is a dynamic creative flow of mind using pure intellect. One uses I-Consciousness to experience situations in the present with alertness and without judgment. One uses intuition and learns the lesson instantaneously. It transforms life. One awakens from illusions. Awareness provides direct wisdom that guides one's life. One does not need to follow any authority. Without awareness, one remains mechanical until one wakes up.

Wisdom: Wisdom is not attained through books or earned through universities. It cannot be bought or sold. It does not come following external authorities, from logic, belief or rejection. A restless and doubting mind is a hindrance to wisdom.

Introspection and awareness while performing any activity produce wisdom. Both pleasant and unpleasant experiences provide wisdom for the future. One experiences revelations from within with awareness during positive and negative experiences. When the mind becomes quiet and receptive and is open to receiving answers, the spark of Atman reflects as intuition and pure intellect follow the guidance.

Ahankar (I-Consciousness): Pure ego and closest to Atman. It is attained when one quiets the mind in deep meditation. It is the foundation and support for the ego.

Ego (Contaminated consciousness): When pure consciousness identifies with any faculty of body, senses, mind or emotions, it becomes contaminated consciousness called ego. The ego is necessary for functioning in the world. Ego is neither good nor bad. If one does not utilize the body, senses and mind for survival or pleasure, one is called Tamasik or lazy. When one becomes a slave to the body, senses and mind, one becomes Rajasik and restless. When one uses body, senses and the mind wisely as a means, one becomes free. One evolves from Tamasik ego to Rajasik ego to Satvik ego and rises above them all. One needs to build an ego gradually. One cultivates ego as strength and self-confidence. One learns spiritual lessons, and finally, the ego drops away. Premature giving up of ego means escape.

Tamasik Ego: It represents lethargy. Laziness is not relaxation. A relaxed person has energy in reserve that can be utilized as necessary, just like a cat that seems motionless until it attacks a mouse. Relaxation vitalizes a person and restores his energy. It also presents ignorance and darkness. It hides the reality with the concealing power of Maya. One does not realize the reality. One has no energy or vitality. One lives the life of an animal with a preoccupation with survival. When Antahkaran awakens, he attains Rajasik state.

Rajasik ego (Restlessness): It is influenced by the projecting power of Maya. It is filled with restless energy. One seeks wealth, pleasure, power and fame. One becomes a slave to wealth, fame and power and suffers. After experiences of many lives, one recognizes errors made and seeks freedom.

Satvik Ego (Pure ego): Purification of antahkaran produces Satvik ego. One becomes successful and content. One chooses the path of Shreya (virtue) and seeks liberation. One becomes a permanent subject of changing body, sense, mind, emotions and the world. One cultivates Vivek and vairagya. One serves selflessly.

Tamasik and Satvik ego look the same: Tamasik ego has not started the journey. One wants all the comforts of life without effort—like a fox who could not reach grapes and declares that grapes are sour. Two parties at a restaurant are sitting without food. One party is hungry and waiting for food, while the other party is waiting for the check.

Gunatit state: One transcends all three states. This is attained when one reaches liberation. One cannot function in this state. There is no mind or duality. An enlightened master and a fool may look alike.

Chapter 3) Vipashyana

Vipashyana is an ancient technique practiced by many spiritual leaders and cultures. Lord Buddha revived the major practice of the Theravada tradition of Buddhism. It is also called the Hinyan (Lower vehicle) of Buddhism. Hinyan Buddhism spread through Southeast Asian countries and almost disappeared from India. Goenka (1924- 2013) was born in Burma to a devout Hindu family. He had serious migraines. He was introduced to the Thervad practice of Vipashyana training, which later healed him. He became a devout follower of Buddhism and started serving the community. He started giving group Vipashyana training with 10-day retreats. The once-forgotten practice of Vipashyana was revived In India by Goenka. His training was widely accepted with great enthusiasm.

Vi means special (vishista) or turn around (viparit). Pashyana means to see or to be aware of. Vipashyana refers to being aware of yourself and looking within the Self (Atman). Vipashyana is also called vipassana in the Pali language, which was spoken in the time of Buddha.

These days, people understand Vipassana as a silent retreat. In reality, a silent retreat involves a simple diet, no phone, music or sense stimulation. One observes Dharma rules along with observation of breath at all times. By being silent and observing the breath, one removes attachments to the body, sense organs and the mind. During the practice, the mind revolts but eventually experiences inner peace. One becomes aware and looks at life with a new perspective.

One should establish personal practice and the practice of mindfulness in normal activities and maintain satsang (gathering of groups for spiritual discourse). One can join a group retreat occasionally for revival.

This book provides Vipashyana practice as passive and active meditations.

Awareness of incoming prana and outgoing apana prepares one for vipashyana. One practices vipashyana of the body, the senses and the mind. Vipashyana of the body can be done in the sitting position only, while vipashyana of the senses and the mind can be done as active meditation also.

One practices awareness of the breath on a daily basis and anytime one remembers. It becomes a habit. One learns to be aware and applies Vipashyana in everyday activities like eating, walking, cooking or talking. Vi also means opposite (viparit). Pashyana means to be aware of. Vipashyana refers to looking within instead of outside.

Two-step practice

1. Anapan sati: Maintain awareness of incoming prana and outgoing apana. This makes the mind quiet and sharp for vipashyana.

2. Vipashyana: (passive observation)

A. Vedna. With a quiet mind, observe sensations and images in the mind (Vedna)

B. Chitta (sanskaras in unconscious mind) During meditation, sanskaras from the unconscious mind are removed.

C. Kaya (Body scan). An entire body scan removes sanskaras stored in the gross body as rudimentary elements (panch maha bhootas) form of earth, water, fire, air and space.

D. Dharma: When one gets freedom from sanskaras, one dwells on Dharma thoughts. It deals with the entire universe and the harmonious flow with life. It dissolves one's own identity.

About the Mind

- The mind is made of thoughts that change every 48 seconds.
- One cannot control the mind; it will rebel.
- Suppressing the mind only makes it restless.
- By focusing the mind on breath, we can break the cycle of the chain reaction of thoughts. The mind can focus on moving breath instead of a single object.
- Breath is constant with us. It is available to us at all times.
- We can utilize the breath while sitting, working and during sleep and dreams.
- When breath slows down, the mind slows down and returns to its source, which is I-Consciousness.
- I-Consciousness is the source of intuition, awareness, inspiration and inner guidance.

Vipashyana to Remove Sanskaras

All experiences of life leave impressions on the unconscious mind (Chitta). There are deep sanskaras from childhood, mother's womb and previous lives. Sanskaras are stored in the subconscious and unconscious mind. The ultimate storage of sanskaras is in the body as five rudimentary elements (Paanch mahabhootas). They are earth, water, fire, air and space. We are controlled by these sanskaras. These sanskaras can be removed from the body, senses and mind through Vipashyana meditation. When all sanskaras are removed, one becomes liberated and free from transmigration.

The body is the field for the functions of all faculties. Sense organs are perceived by the mind and follow the mind's command. The mind only holds information and records it. The intellect makes judgments on this information. I-Consciousness is the only subject of experience. I-Consciousness is the observer, and Atman is the witness. When I-Consciousness identifies with objects of experience, it gets enmeshed in Maya (cosmic illusion). One interprets experiences as pleasant or unpleasant and craves to repeat the pleasant. All impressions are stored in the unconscious mind (Chitta) as memories. Memories and desires compel one to rebirth. This is considered bondage. One can escape karma and sanskaras if one remains as an instrument instead of being a doer.

Patanjali's Samadhi to Remove Sanskaras

There are four lower states of samadhi and ultimate samadhi (nirbij). Nirbij samadhi means total extinction of the ego. During Vipashyana practice, meditation and basic Samadhi remove gross sanskaras. Subtler sanskaras are removed during deeper Samadhi. When all sanskaras are removed, one has no more desires to fulfill and no need to sustain a body. One merges with Supreme Consciousness. This is called liberation. One becomes free.

Vipashyana Process of Releasing Sanskaras

Awareness uses I-consciousness, which harmonizes with Chitta (mind) using Prana (energy). One remains a passive witness to release sanskaras. During deep meditation, impressions from chitta flow to the astral and gross bodies and are released. This is the release of sanskaras.

1. Astral body: When sanskaras flow to the astral body, it produces pleasant and unpleasant sensations and visions. The sensations may be of attraction or repulsion. Observe them with neutral awareness. Welcome them. Observe them without reaction, likes, or dislikes—like watching a movie. The sanskaras will disappear when viewed by a passive, choiceless observer.

2. Gross body: Sanskaras flow to the gross body. Sanskaras are released as microscopic rudimentary elements of earth, water, fire, air and space. These releases produce sensations within the body. One may experience various sensations at gross and subtle levels. The sensations come as pressure, tightness, tingling, vibrations, heat, cold or fluidity.

They may be painful, pleasant or neutral. The sensations can be felt inside or outside the body. They may connect with different areas of the body or may connect with the mind and emotions. These sensations arise and pass away. Nothing remains permanent. Their nature is impermanence (Anitya). Nothing is eternal except Atman.

Maintain equanimity and perceive the release of sanskaras as an observer (Drishta). Remain open and receptive to feelings of love and compassion. Do not judge, analyze, or react. Reacting will reinforce the impression. Hidden sanskaras in the Chitta create disturbances in your life. They are like trapped gases at the bottom of a reservoir that bubble up to the surface. When all the gases are released, the reservoir becomes quiet again. Sensations felt in the body are the bubbles of sanskaras. When hidden sanskaras are removed, we become free and enjoy life fully. We become childlike, unleashed from programming.

Application of Vipashyana

The techniques of Vipashyana were developed over a period of 4,000 years. All the techniques are very similar and were suitable at their time in history. One should not compare them and judge them from the perspective of our current age.

We should adopt a dynamic approach to go within ourselves and choose our own path. We must be free to adopt whatever technique suits us best.

We can use yoga positions and breathing techniques as a means. However, we must keep our ultimate goal in mind and stay on the path while being free to change the means as necessary.

Utilizing the Raja yoga of Patanjali

Raja yoga of Patanjali is the most systematic and scientific path.

Foundation:

Harmonious living is the foundation. One has to be in rhythm with nature and flow with it. Animals follow rhythm due to their fundamental instinct for survival. If one is not in rhythm, exercises, nutrition, breathing and meditation will fail to provide results. Yama and Niyama are the foundation.

1. Yama means restraint of basic instincts of violence, untruth, stealing, sexual preoccupation, and greed.

2. Niyama means cultivating positive qualities like purity, austerity, contentment, self-study, and surrender.

Gross body (Ground floor):

The basic tool for inquiring about the Self. It is the instrument that supports the senses, mind, intellect and consciousness. The practice of Hatha Yoga makes one strong enough to withstand hardships. Hatha yoga refers to balancing positive (Sun) and negative (Moon) energy. Yoga positions, breathing, nutrition and internal cleansing techniques are used to build and support the foundation of a healthy body.

3. Asana are the Yoga positions that manage the nervous system, endocrine system, circular system and muscular system

4. Pranayamas are breathing techniques for nurturing the lungs and balancing and purifying astral nerves (Nadis). There are pranayamas to generate body heat, relax and slow down nerve functions and balance the nervous system for meditation.

Astral body (First floor)

5. Pratyahara (sense withdrawal) is restraining the five sense organs from external stimulations.

6. Dharana (concentration) focuses all restrained energy at one point.

Causal body (Second floor)

7. Dhyana (meditation) is the continuous flow of concentration.

8. Samadhi (Absorption) includes four lower samadhi and a final Nirbij Samadhi. During lower samadhi, the gross sanskaras are removed by vipashyana practice. In seedless Samadhi, the ego is destroyed, and subtle sanskaras are removed. One is liberated.

The Threefold Path

1. Utilize dynamic, intuitive moral conduct that harmonizes life with the universal rhythm (dharma).

2. Quiet and sharpen the mind by observing the breath.

3. Be both Drishta (passive observer) and Sakshi (witness). Being a passive observer means maintaining choiceless awareness. Pure consciousness observes the changing material universe and remains untouched by it. This leads one to be a witness—the ultimate unified observer of everything. Duality dissolves. There is only one consciousness. It pervades and vivifies all things.

Chapter 4) Practices for Self-Inquiry

This chapter includes various practices that center on vipashyana and the awareness of breath for self-inquiry.

Vipashyana in Passive Meditation

- Sit in any comfortable and steady position or lie down on the floor.
- Travel with incoming and outgoing breath.
- Do not try to control the breath.
- Accept the breath as is.
- Let go of all resistance and feel comfortable with your environment.
- Turn all sensations into calming experiences.
- Allow your breath to slow down and become rhythmic.
- Allow the practice to be effortless and increase it with love.
- Experience yourself as Atman observing the breath.
- Feel your existence apart from your breath.
- Feel your existence apart from your body.

- Feel your existence apart from external sensations.
- Feel your existence apart from changing thoughts and emotions.
- Your existence is a constant subject.
- You observe everything outside as a changing object.

Variation:

- After success in the basic practice, you can try the variation below.
- Continue observing the breath as before.
- Be aware of the subtlety of the breath.
- Observe the end part of the breath. It becomes subtler and stops for a microsecond before making the transition. It happens at both ends of the breath.
- During that short suspension of breath, your mind enters a suspended state and gives you deep peace.
- Experience both ends of breath merging and experience bliss.

Vipashyana in Active Meditation

Practice awareness of incoming prana and outgoing apana on a daily basis and whenever you get a chance. It will become a habit within a few days to be able to maintain the rhythm of the breath at all times.

You will be able to apply active meditation to any situation in life effortlessly. Apply the technique in passive or active meditation during the day.

- Feel your existence apart from the constantly changing body.
- Feel your existence apart from the constantly changing sensations.
- Feel your existence apart from the constantly changing thoughts.
- Feel your existence apart from the constantly changing emotions.
- Experience Atman as permanent and real, and everything else is impermanent.

Example of Vipashyana While Walking

One gets into the habit of walking unconsciously while restless thoughts and worries race through one's mind. One can walk slowly with awareness. One can pay attention to each step, reaching the floor, touching the floor, and the next foot rising. Slowing down and paying attention will keep you in the present and will revive you. Your normal walking activity will turn into meditation.

Example of Vipashyana While Practicing Yoga Positions

First, visualize the yoga positions you want to practice. Let go of mental control and practice the routine extremely slowly while being in the present. Leave the mind alone as an observer. As you continue, you will experience the effect of gravity. Observe your body as it goes through various moves. Be aware of incoming breath with backward bends and outgoing breath with forward bends. Experience the deeper organs and muscles with the depth of each breath. Feel the biofeedback with the nervous system, mind and emotions. The entire process becomes like a dance. Remain as an observer of the flowing dance.

Example of Vipashyana While Eating

One slows down the activity of eating. One becomes aware of each moment and experiences it. One becomes aware of hunger in the stomach, and one feels the sensation of the chair. One watches oneself taking utensils, reaching for food, the sensation of food in the mouth, chewing the food, awareness of taste, food swallowed down the throat and feels the stomach filling up with the food. One remains alert and aware, takes a long time to eat, and learns to apply it in other areas of life. This may take a long time and may not be practical.

You can apply this technique to make it more practical. Eat slowly with awareness. Chew the food and savor it. You will be satisfied with less food and get more joy from eating for a longer time. It will promote undereating, which makes for better digestion and health. Eat quietly without talking, thinking, worrying or rushing.

Example of Vipashyana During Interactions

You talk to others and interact with them. Observe the breath. Listen to others and do not react to their positive or negative comments. You will not react impulsively and react in a way that you may regret later on. You will be able to interact constructively instead.

Vipashyana While Shopping or Making Choices

Observe the breath, come into the present and be rooted in the Self before making hasty decisions. Try to maintain your balance before impulses get hold of you. Do not let your desires take control. Do not be impressed by salespeople or flashy commercials. Be visionary and think of the long-term consequences of your choices and decisions. Postpone the decision for a day, and you will gain the wisdom to make a proper choice. By observing the breath, the impulse dies away.

Thoughts and emotions change constantly while you remain as a permanent observer or witness. If you get rooted within the Self, you will remain the master of your life.

Vipashyana During Disease or Suffering

Pain is natural and should be accepted. Resistance to pain magnifies the suffering. Observe the breath and create distance from pain. When you remain an observer of pain, it will subside.

Create distance from your pain. When the distance increases, pain reduces to that extent. Most of the pain is magnified due to memories.

Vipashyana During Stress, Anger, Fear or Anxiety

Observe the breath and observe emotions. Emotions come and go and change constantly. You are not your thoughts or emotions. Create separation instead of identity with the emotions. Observe emotions like watching them on the movie screen. When you expand your consciousness, your emotions will lose their intensity. When you increase love and compassion for others, your preoccupation with yourself will dissipate.

Entire Body Scan

Body scanning involves using point systems throughout your body and traveling from point to point. Breathe in and out, staying at the same point for three breaths. Observe the sensations felt in the surrounding area with equanimity. Sensations come and go. Observe without judging them. You may experience heat, cold, fluidity, stretch, or burning. The sanskaras leave as you observe the sensations. Sensations are from five rudimentary elements of earth, water, fire and air working in space. You feel relief from sanskaras.

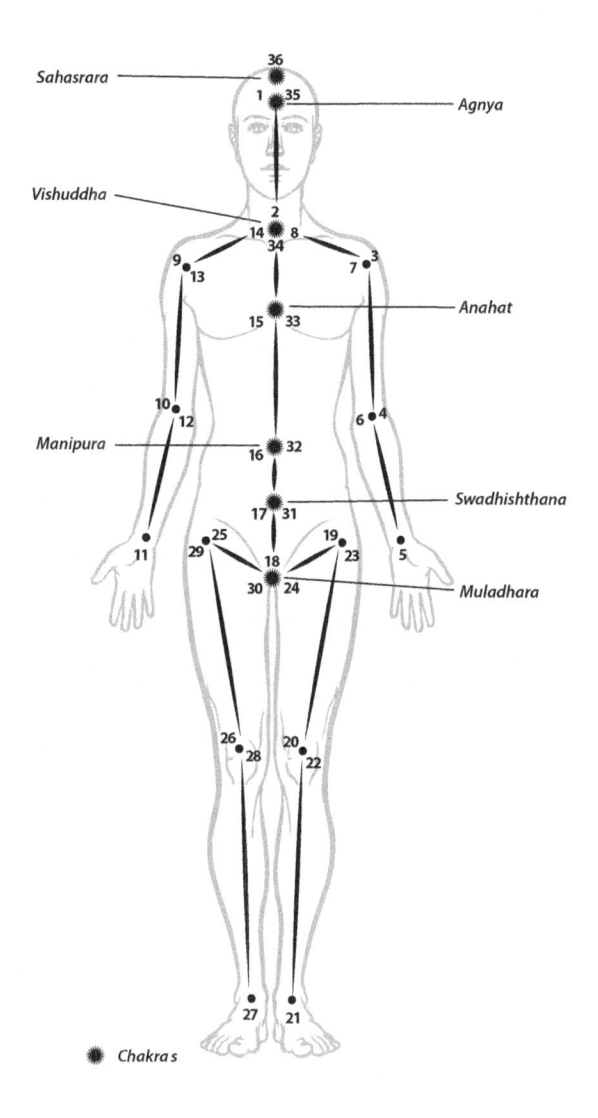

Chakras

The journey starts from the third eye.

- Lie comfortably on your back with your eyes closed. Loosen your neck, shake your arms and legs and let them relax. Start the mental travel from head to toe and return from toe to head, covering each part of your body: head, face, neck, throat, left shoulder, arms, forearms, hands, and fingers. Return and go to the right shoulder to the entire right arm and back to the throat.
- Travel through the chakras to the Muladhara chakra.
- Then, travel to the left hip, knees, ankle and toes. Return back and repeat the travel through your right leg. Return to points of Kundalini and escape through the thousand petal lotus at the top of the head.
- It may take you a total of twenty to thirty minutes to complete the journey. You may take whatever time is necessary. Keep your awareness on each small area for one minute or longer, observing neutrally with awareness. Be aware of all sensations without judgment. Sensations may come with the release of the sanskaras. Continue moving forward to the next area. Sometimes, you may get stuck, go into a swoon, get lost, or fall asleep. Do not worry, and do not judge. It is part of the learning process, and you will go deeper with repetition on a regular basis. There is no failure. There is

no goal. The practice itself is the goal, and the reward of peace and wisdom is built into the practice. Stay in the blissful state to savor the experience. The entire body scan can be used as a deep relaxation technique or technique to fall asleep.

Quick Body Scan

When you master the technique, you can scan your entire body with three breaths. Allow awareness to travel with the breath and scan the body. The entire body can be scanned quickly by traveling through the body using the three breaths with awareness.

1. The first breath goes in through the nostrils and travels from the third eye to the throat center. Hold it for a moment and travel through shoulders, arms, palms and fingertips as you slowly release the breath through the mouth. Remain aware of the sensations.

2. During the second breath, you breathe in through all your fingers and both thumbs to the throat center. Hold it for a moment and travel through the trunk, hips, legs, ankles, feet and toes with the release of the breath. Experience the sensations.

3. During the third breath, you inhale through the toes to the base of the spine. Hold it for a moment

and travel the inner path of the spine, touching all centers of kundalini (chakras) and escape through the thousand-petal lotus at the top of the head with your exhale. Expand and merge with cosmic consciousness. Repeat all three steps, allowing the sanskaras to release naturally. Stay in the blissful state to savor the experience.

Identity With the Breath

Identity with the breath is the practice of being the breath instead of observing the breath. This practice is useful to achieve absorption and dissolve the mind. One can use this technique during passive sitting meditation only. One can apply this practice before going to sleep, and one will remain in meditation during sleep and dreams.

Technique: Become the Breath

- Sit in any comfortable and steady position or lie down on the floor.
- Travel with incoming and outgoing breath.
- Do not try to control the breath.
- Merge with the breath and become the breath.
- Let the breath slow down and become rhythmic.
- Experience your being changing with the breath.
- Continue for 5 minutes and become passive, letting go of resistance.

- Accept everything without resistance. Accept noises, discomforts and thoughts.
- Remain a passive observer and turn distractions into support.
- Increase the practice as you enjoy it, and it will become effortless.
- Observe the transition of your breath and the end part of your breath.
- There is a suspension of breath before and after the breath.
- Observe that your mind slows down with subtle breath and is suspended when your breath stops.
- This is the transcendental state of mind and the experience of pure consciousness.

Practice regularly in the morning. Also, practice this technique before going to sleep. The technique will continue during sleep and dreams.

Technique: Expand and Become Homogeneous

Atman is located in the innermost chamber of the heart. Its energy flows through 101 astral nerve channels of the body. It branches further into 72,000 nadis (astral channels) throughout the entire body. It expands in space and becomes universal Brahman.

- Begin by sitting in a steady position.
- Observe the breath passively.

- Accept your environment without resistance.
- Feel that the body is porous and all pores of the skin are breathing along with nostrils.
- Travel in with the breath and go to the spiritual heart (Atman) located in the middle of the chest.
- Feel the natural attraction and become introverted to merge with Atman.
- Retain the breath for a short time naturally and experience the divine glow of healing light, love, and compassion.
- During the short retention, feel the radiant light healing your entire being.
- With passive, gentle, outgoing breath through the mouth, allow the healing light to spread throughout the body, pushing out all impurities and expanding to infinity.
- Continue the practice by experiencing incoming and outgoing breath-like waves.
- Feel the disintegration of your body and remain as consciousness, expand and become homogeneous.
- Repeat the process and remain blissful.

Chapter 5) Simplified Guidance

We are asleep and do not know it. A dream looks real until we wake up. We are under the influence of Maya. This is a waking dream. A waking dream is longer than a dream; everyone participates in this dream, and it looks more permanent. However, there is a supreme reality that is the permanent transcendental reality during dreams and waking. When we wake up to the supreme reality, we become free. When we wake up, we recognize that the world is a relative reality. We live in the world like short-time travelers and perform our duties without attachments. We perform our duties wholeheartedly, like an actor on stage. We find peace and freedom in proportion to waking up.

Ten Steps to Waking Up

1. Become Empty

One has to be empty and open to receive new guidance. The cup has to be empty to receive new contents. Valleys fill up with water while mountaintops remain dry. One has to be humble to receive wisdom from a master. Subtle ego produces hindrance to humility. We are filled with old information and conditioning. We have to slow down from the bombardment of information. We have to turn information into knowledge and wisdom. We have to store wisdom as sanskaras that guide us for life.

2. Think Clearly

One needs to think clearly. To think clearly, you have to let go of external authorities and rely on yourself. The mind is filled with insecurity, fear, anger, expectation, and confusion, and it cannot think clearly. One has to be quiet and remove all past conditions and programming. One has to let go of all self-imposed conditions for being happy. One only needs food, shelter and clothing. One can be happy with a simpler life. As a matter of fact, one finds happiness with fewer possessions. Extra comforts and luxuries have been a curse for the most part. One has become lazy, dependent and intolerant of others. One's consciousness has become narrow, and the mind is occupied with self-protection, fears, and worries. With a contaminated mind, one cannot see the reality.

3. Think Out of the Box

Many people are totally brainwashed by their upbringing, schooling, religion, social media and computers. One cannot think creatively. New discoveries are made by people who can think, dream and visualize. A hypothesis is necessary for any research. We accomplish what we can visualize clearly. We have to expand our consciousness. Science fiction of the past has become the reality of today.

4. Make a Quantum Leap

Everyone has a chance to make a quantum leap. A quantum leap bypasses all the normal steps and is like taking an elevator to the top floor. We can awaken the potential within us. When energy is focused, and wisdom shows us the proper direction, we can make a quantum leap. Like an observer who turns waves of possibilities into a particle, we can choose and project reality. The undercurrent of our inner personality leads us to make a quantum leap.

5. Attain Wisdom

Wisdom is hidden deep within us. It comes from within as a personal revelation. When the mind becomes quiet and receptive and open to receive, intuition answers. The spark of Atman reflects as intuition and pure intellect follows the guidance.

Wisdom is also attained by the practice of mindfulness and awareness. By being aware and alert during direct experience, one can learn lessons and accumulate knowledge.

Generally, one becomes wiser with age because of various experiences in life. One lives with awareness, practices introspection and sets priorities in life. One attains a surplus of health, money, time, and energy. One gains the wisdom to balance life, becoming happy and content. When one awakens to higher awareness and becomes content, one uses their material life as a means to attain spiritual wisdom and self-realization. One grows in wisdom with age and finds greater joy in life instead of suffering.

People who live without awareness get attached to material possessions and ambitions. They become possessive of family members and friends instead of loving them unconditionally. Such persons worry about the future and experience insecurity, fear, loneliness and suffering.

6. Set Priorities

Use wisdom in setting priorities. Time and life, in general, get wasted if there is no priority. With priority, we save time and energy. Setting priorities is like looking at a map. One can choose the inward path to lasting happiness instead of the outward journey to suffering. One should prioritize yearly goals. One should set a priority for each day. Visualize the tasks ahead of time. You can accomplish many tasks in a single trip. Priorities should not be rigid. Changes can be made and altered with changing situations. It is similar to a GPS system that resets directions towards the destination. Flow with life and enjoy life.

7. Prevent Sanskaras

The law of karma means that all causes produce subsequent results until exhausted. Each action produces a chain reaction. We produce karma with thoughts, speech, and physical activities. The result may come in any combination of physical or mental manifestations and can be immediate or delayed. Sanskaras are mostly produced by an impure ego that uses the mind, intention and desire to achieve external results. They are produced by being a doer. Deeper sanskaras are produced by attachment. But if we perform our actions without being a doer or work as an instrument of God, we become free from sanskaras even when we do external activities. We produce more karmas and sanskaras with thoughts than physical activities. Use your eyes to see the divinity in all, use your ears to listen to the glories of God, use your hands to serve others and give to charities. See no evil, hear no evil and speak no evil.

Serving selflessly does not produce sanskaras.

8. *Vipashyana to Remove Sanskaras*

During Vipashyana practice, meditation and basic Samadhi remove gross sanskaras. Subtler sanskaras are removed during deeper Samadhi. When all sanskaras are removed, one has no more desires to fulfill and no need to attain a body. One merges with Supreme Consciousness. This is called liberation.

When we practice breathing to quiet the intellect, our gross, astral and causal bodies harmonize with Chitta (mind) using Prana (energy). During deep meditation, impressions from chitta flow to the astral and gross bodies and are released. This is the release of sanskaras.

When sanskaras flow to the astral body, pleasant and unpleasant sensations and visions are produced. The sensations may be of attraction or repulsion. Observe them with neutral awareness. Welcome them. Use them to remove old conditioning.

Finally, the sanskaras flow to the gross body. Sanskaras are released as microscopic rudimentary elements of earth, water, fire, air and space. These releases produce sensations within the body. One may experience various sensations at gross and subtle levels. The sensations come as pressure, tightness, tingling, vibrations, heat, cold, fluidity, grossness, or flow. They may be painful, pleasant or neutral. They may be felt inside or outside the body. They may connect with different areas of the body or with the mind and emotions. These sensations arise and pass away. Nothing remains permanent. Their nature is impermanence (Anitya). Nothing is eternal except Atman. Maintain equanimity and perceive the release of sanskaras as an observer (Drishta). Remain open and receptive to feelings of love and compassion. Do not judge, analyze, or react. Reacting will reinforce the impression. Hidden sanskaras in the chitta create disturbances in your life. They are like trapped gases at the bottom of a reservoir that bubble up to the surface. When all the gases are released, the reservoir becomes quiet again. Sensations felt in the body are the bubbles of sanskaras. When hidden sanskaras are removed, we become free and enjoy life fully. We become childlike, unleashed from programming.

9. Be an Observer or a Witness

The body is the field for the functions of all faculties. Sense organs are perceived by the mind. Motor organs follow the mind's command. The mind only records information. Intellect makes judgments. I-Conscious is the only subject of experience. I-Consciousness is the observer, and Atman is the witness. When I-Consciousness identifies with objects of experience, it gets into Maya (cosmic illusions). One interprets experiences as pleasant or unpleasant and craves to repeat them. All the impressions are stored in the unconscious mind (Chitta) as memories. These memories and desires compel one to rebirth. This transmigration is considered bondage.

Observer (Drishta): I-Consciousness is constant without past, future and judgments. One becomes an observer of the body, perceptions, thoughts and emotions. One remains as a subject of all changing objects. One remains apart as an observer and does not get tangled with thoughts and emotions.

Witness (Sakshi): When the observer observes one's own self, the illusion of personal self disappears. Only one universal self remains.

10. *Turn Life Into Meditation*

Meditation is living with awareness. Practice all activities with mindfulness and awareness.
Turn your house into a temple and your job and business as service to the Lord. Turn your social life into Satsang. Turn each breath into a reminder of Self. Remember "So" with each incoming breath and "Hum" with each outgoing breath. The mantra "So Hum" becomes a constant reminder of Self. Use your sense organs, motor organs and mind to serve others selflessly. This will dissolve the ego.

Contemplation for Eternal Bliss

1. Suffering: Life is filled with pain and suffering. Pleasure, pain and bliss are relative and fluctuate constantly.

2. Personal gain: People are in illusion and think that pleasure comes by attaining wealth, success, fame or power. In reality, it comes in proportion to losing ego, identity, or attachments. Joy comes in proportion to the loss of ego.

3. Mind is the cause of all sufferings: Suffering is an illusion and is created in the mind. The intensity of pleasure and pain can be changed by the mind. Great joy comes as a result of contentment. To master the mind, we first master the breath, to observe it either as an observer or being one with the breath by being the breath.

4. The mind cannot be controlled by force: Force disturbs the mind. The simplest method of controlling the mind is to tame it by mastering the breath.

5. Selfless service: Remove unconscious anger and spread compassion for all living creatures. This does not make you weak, a coward, or an escapist. It will give you joy and liberation. You do not need to belong to any religion, follow any Guru or follow any austerity. Simply perform your duty to all

living creatures, to nature, and to society. The work itself will provide the greatest reward.

6. Unconditional love: It is the remedy for the world today, and it is the teaching of all the masters.

7. Simplify life: We need only food, shelter and clothing. We have created problems by extending our needs to wants and desires, and we have developed compulsive addictions to greed, ego, and exhibition.

8. Surplus: Develop a surplus of time, money, energy and wisdom. Wisdom will come last and is the hardest to obtain.

9. Loneliness: We are alone from birth til death, and we run our entire life searching.

Buddha teaches that all life is suffering and shows us the way to end suffering. Vedanta teaches that our essence is bliss and shows us the way to attain bliss. Both are correct. Buddha gives us the beginning, and Vedanta gives us the end, but both suffering and bliss are an illusion. Suffering is an illusion, and happiness is an illusion—not knowing the truth is the problem.

We are all interconnected. Anything bad you do to the world, you do to yourself. We must remove anger and develop compassion, stillness, and no-mind.

Meditation Techniques to Experience Bliss

Bliss is our basic nature. Due to ignorance, we feel bound. Our basic nature is existence, consciousness and bliss. We go through three states of consciousness: waking, dreaming and deep sleep. We believe them as reality due to ignorance. We are eternal consciousness during all these states. In reality, when we transcend all the lower states, we can experience our basic nature.

Meditation awakens us to direct experience. Mind cannot be controlled, but it can be managed. When the mind is totally quiet, we experience our divine nature. Meditation practices are meant to transcend the mind.

Perception

- Sit comfortably or lie down in a comfortable position. Breathe naturally and continue until it becomes effortless.
- Focus on the incoming and outgoing breath. Allow it to become natural, effortless and enjoyable. Flow passively with incoming and outgoing breath.
- With incoming breath, experience prana passively entering your heart center, and with out-

going breath, prana leaving the body. Deep-rooted tensions are hidden in the body. They are removed by forgiveness. Prayers and love produce healing. The following technique heals and increases 1 and 2 heals and cultivates love for all.

Meditation to Release Deep-Rooted Tensions

- Incoming breath: repentance of everything done to others by thoughts, words and actions.
- Outgoing breath: Release and allow it to evaporate. Visualize.
- Practice in the morning and at the end of the day. Practice temperance to others so as not to accumulate any sanskaras. By forgiving yourself, you purify yourself. As you forgive others, your body and mind will start healing. Remove deep-rooted anger and rage while you are doing the practice. Invisible anger is anger we are not aware of that can accumulate over the years, especially during the growing years. When those angers are removed, they are healed immediately.
- Anger from growing years in hidden form causes problems in the present. In the evening, practice going over all the things that have accumulated and all the mistakes that were made so you forgive yourself and recharge yourself so that you don't repeat the mistakes.

Meditation for Deeper Healing

- Inhale with thoughts of love and compassion to your neighbors.
- Breathe in with their mental image, and fill them with love and compassion. Breathe out and connect with compassion.
- Repeat until the experience gets established. Start with loved ones, then strangers, and finally, reach out to the people you dislike. Move on to all living beings, the animal kingdom and nature. Do not start a new project until you cultivate deep mental compassion in your mind. Remember to forgive yourself for mistakes you have made so you can continue with enthusiasm.

Meditation to Transcend the Koshas

In the ancient scripture *Taitirya Upanishad*, a father directs his son to liberation. He guides him in understanding karta bhokta (doer-enjoyer), to neti neti (not this, not that), and finally, to the observer, Atman. He guides his son from gross to subtle to causal until he finds liberation. The path of liberation is in our basic nature and has to be recovered.

The five koshas: physical body (annamaya kosha), breath body (pranamaya kosha), emotional body (manomaya kosha), intellectual body (vijnanmaya kosha), bliss body (anandamaya kosha).

- Breathe in and focus on the first kosha, the physical body, the annamaya kosha, and recognize that you are the observer and not the thought.
- Stay for a while until you experience yourself as pure and eternal consciousness. Not touched or controlled by the annamaya kosha. Repeat for the other four koshas and become free from all the manifestations of the five sheaths, the five bodies. We can strengthen our conviction that we are only instrumental for the time being. Pleasure and pain are temporary. They come and go. We can become masters of our thoughts, speech, and actions. We can influence others with our speech, thoughts and presence.
- During the day, practice and remain aware that you are the observer.
- Breathe out. This practice will turn into an effortless habit.

Inspiration and Guidance for Living

The following is a combination of definitions and concepts. They are meant to be studied subjectively. Use them for introspection and daily guidance.

Abhyas and Vairagya: These two disciplines are recommended by Lord Krishna and Yogi Patanjali for sincere seekers. Abhyas means sustained practice, and Vairagya means renunciation of the results. It refers to patience and perseverance. Its essence is to sustain steadiness in practice during misfortune, temptation, irritation, annoyance, restlessness, or laziness.

Acceptance: Accept the changing nature of everyone and everything in the world. Let go of all expectations from everyone. Accept old age, disease and death as a reality of life. Renounce and find instant peace.

Aloneness: Aloneness is being connected with the Self. It is always peaceful. Loneliness is being disconnected from the Self and searching outside for peace. We are alone from birth until death. No one can do anything for us, and we cannot do anything for others. We can only support others. A hungry person has to eat himself. It is a lonely journey. We forget this and accumulate possessions and loved ones and get attached to them. We regret it in the end.

Ahankar (I-Consciousness): I-Consciousness is the spark of Atman. Expand your consciousness. Joy and freedom grow in proportion to your consciousness. If you identify yourself with any faculty of body, mind or emotion, you shrink your consciousness. This produces limitations and bondage.

Antahakaran: Antahkaran is our true inner personality. It is the combination of mind, intellect, and unconscious mind. I-consciousness directs them.

Atman (Self): Atman's nature is eternal bliss consciousness. Be quiet and introverted to experience it. Searching for happiness from the world or others is an extroverted activity that will result in suffering.

Aum: Aum is a sacred symbol that represents Brahman (Supreme consciousness). It covers three states of consciousness: Jagrat (Waking), Swapna (Dream) and Susupti (deep sleep).
It is the Bija (root) Mantra and is the essence of all Mantras. It is the sound of the universe.

Advaita: Non-dual. There is only one reality, and everyone is interconnected. Separate existence is an illusion. Advaita is an ancient philosophy and is validated by quantum physics.

Balance and Surplus: Attaining a surplus of energy, money, and time gives you freedom in life and reduces stress. Balance these with wisdom. Use material success as a means to the spiritual path. Practice and balance the path of Gnana, Karma and Bhakti yoga. They balance knowledge, activities and devotion.

Charity begins at home: We are the starting point. We can help ourselves first before helping others. Do not entertain any negative thoughts. Thoughts are real. Affirm positive thoughts; they become reality in time.

Choices: We have the choice to choose the path of Preya (pleasure) and get trapped in the world. Or we can choose the path of Sreya (virtue) toward liberation. Choices are made by purity of antahkaran and awareness.

Contentment: Contentment is the climax of true success. One's desires are fulfilled. A wet cloth does not absorb any more moisture. One enjoys being here and now.

Desires: There are three desires that can trap human beings:

1. Vitteshana (Desire for wealth)
2. Lokeshana (Fame and power)
3. Putrshana (Desire for progeny)

Dharma: Dharma is duties. We remain healthy and happy by following the rhythm of nature. Animals use instinct, while humans have to use pure intellect to follow the universal rhythm. Perform your Dharma to serve the Lord. Give up expectations of rewards. Gracefully accept the results as blessings (prasad) of the Lord.

Drishta (Observer): Remember that you are the constant subject to see and experience is constantly changing universe. Observe everything, like watching images on a movie screen. You will not be deluded. You will remain the peaceful master of yourself.

Duality: Duality means two. Two opposites are hidden within each other like two sides of a coin. One can transcend duality by maintaining inner tranquility. Mind is the cause of duality. Pleasure-pain, success-failure, and gain-loss are the cycles of duality. Slow down the mind or transcend the mind to rise above duality. Awareness can remove duality.

Effort and grace: Perform your duties (Dharma) and surrender results to the grace of the Almighty. God's grace showers on us all the time—be ready to receive it. Plant the seeds first and wait for the rain.

Freedom and discipline: Disciplines are built in freedom. Perform your duty (Dharma) and surrender the results to receive the grace of God. The speed of a car is freedom, while steering and brakes are the disciplines. The discipline of saving gives freedom to spend. Building a dam provides the freedom to produce channels for agriculture.

Freedom and bondage: Bondage means restriction of time and space. Transmigration, or being born over and over again, is considered bondage (bandhan). Freedom refers to expansion in time and space. It refers to the extinction of all signs and attainment of eternal peace and bliss (mukti).

Ego (Ahankar): Ahankar is a pure consciousness. Covered by three qualities (Gunas), it becomes contaminated. One needs to build an ego to cultivate self-confidence and then become humble. One evolves from laziness to activity to purity.

Flow with life: Life is like an ocean with waves, currents, and wind. Be like a sailboat and use them to your advantage. There are four kinds of categories of people in the world, according to Yogi Patanjali:

1. Sukhi (Happy): Join them
2. Dukhi (Unhappy): Have compassion for them.
3. Punyatma (Virtous): Take delight in them
4. Papatma (Wicked): Avoid them and be indifferent to them

Forgiveness: Forgiveness removes burdens and physical and psychological diseases. Repentance removes sanskaras. Rage gets locked in the body and the mind. It harms one physically and mentally. Forgiveness produces instant relief. Forgive yourself and correct your mistakes instead of feeling guilty.

Goal-direction: Having a goal produces anxiety. Staying on the path gives you the freedom to enjoy your journey. Stay on the path and enjoy your journey toward the goal. Change the means as necessary.

Gratitude: Gratitude allows you to appreciate life and attainments. It expands consciousness and joy. Feel gratitude for life instead of complaining.

Guru: A person who leads you from the darkness of ignorance to the light of wisdom is Guru. A true Guru serves selflessly to awaken your inner Guru.

Help and service: Help involves ego. It wants some rewards and produces bondage. Service is selfless. It expands your consciousness and brings freedom.

Humility: Humility means being lower to receive. The ego is a hindrance to humility. Mountaintops remain dry while valleys fill with water. Tall trees are destroyed in a storm, while small, flexible trees bend and survive. Spiritual wisdom is transferred from a Guru to a disciple when the disciple becomes humble and surrenders.

Introversion-Extroversion: Introversion is the true source of lasting happiness. Extroversion and attraction to the world provide a temporary sense of pleasure followed by bondage and suffering.

Karma and Sanskara: The Law of Karma is a universal law of cause and effect. We perform actions with thoughts, speech and activities. All activities produce results, chain reactions and impressions in the unconscious mind (Sanskaras). Sanskaras control our lives.

Jagat (Sansara): Jagat is the material universe. It is relatively real during limited time and space. Since it is constantly changing, it is called Sansasa. It is also called Maya or cosmic illusion.

Jivatma (Soul): Pure Atman, covered by the ignorance of Maya, forgets its true nature and is called Jivatma. Atman identifies itself with the mind, intellect, and unconscious mind and becomes Jivatma. Jivatma can wake up from Maya and become Atman.

Love and attachments: Love is unconditional and expands our consciousness. Love gets polluted with attachments. Attachments control and disturb our peace. Attachments are created due to subtle ego and desire to control others. Unconditional love can remove attachments.

Macrocosm and microcosm: Entire universe is called Brahmand (Macrocosm). All living creatures are called Pinda (Microcosm). Both are alike. All living creatures are like the thread of a cloth of the universe. Studying one crystal of salt reveals an understanding of all salts.

Master or slave: The Master controls while a slave is controlled. Our mind makes us master or slave. One who uses his senses wisely remains a master. A moth dies due to the attraction of light, a fish dies due to the attraction to taste, a snake dies due to the attraction to sound, a bee dies due to the attraction to smell, and an elephant dies due to the attraction to touch.

Mauna (Inner silence): Mauna is inner silence. One is removed from the world by withdrawing senses. One withdraws chitta from corresponding objects of the senses. One experiences lasting peace. Mauna is a spiritual discipline recommended to preserve energy.

Maya: Maya is a cosmic illusion. Due to Maya, the transient world looks real and binds. The same Maya can become a tool for liberation.

Moderation: Moderation is the middle path to success and happiness. Indulgence produces guilt, suppression, and indulgence once again. String instruments work best when moderately stretched.

Needs, wants, desires, cravings: Need is the starting point. It grows to wants, desires and cravings. It makes one a slave.

Pain and suffering: Pain is a reality of life. Resistance to pain or dwelling on pain produces suffering. Pain can be reduced by passively observing it and creating distance from it.

Peace: Peace is our basic nature. Be still and experience it. Searching for peace only creates noise.

Perfection: You are perfect as you are here and now. Go within and realize your essential nature is eternal bliss. There is nothing to do, nowhere to go and nothing to be.

Prana: Prana is universal energy. It governs the entire universe and all living creatures. Prana enters our body at birth and departs at death. By mastering prana, one can control universal forces and can heal. Prana is closest to us and available to us at all times. We can use prana to control the mind and get the mastery of the Self.

Prayer, meditation, surrender: Prayer is talking to God, meditation is listening to God, and surrender is obeying God.

Purity: Purity starts with the purity of the body. Deeper and subtler purification is mental. Still deeper is the purity of intellect and unconscious mind. Yoga practices can purify the body and the mind. Deep meditation and vipashyana can purify the unconscious mind.

Purusharth (Attainments): Four attainments in human life are wealth, pleasure, dharma and moksha. Wealth and pleasure last for a short time and do not survive death. Practice moral acts (Dharma) and work toward liberation (Moksha) while earning wealth and pleasure. These are the only worthwhile attainable accomplishments. They bring joy while living and survive death.

Sakshi (Witness): Witness means a passive observer untouched by anything. It is like space that contains everything, yet is not touched by flood or fire and not divided. It is like a mirror that reflects everything in front as it is. One becomes homogeneous with all living creatures.

Samata: Samata means mental tranquility. Samata means mastery of the dualistic emotions of pleasure-pain, which waste energy and disturb peace. One remains steady, like the center of a wheel.

Sanskara: All outer experiences leave pleasant and unpleasant impressions on the unconscious mind (chitta). These are called sanskaras. Sanskaras can be positive or negative and control our lives.

Satsang: Associations that revive us on our path are called satsang. AA and Weight Watchers are examples. For spiritual revival, one can also benefit from group meetings. The group meeting provides collective energy to persons who need it, like a forest fire that burns green trees with dry trees. Lord Buddha recommended three refuges as satsang:

1. Dharna
2. Enlightened persons
3. Sangha (gathering of monks)

Seclusion: Seclusion is for revival. External seclusion is to be away from crowded places. True seclusion is to restrain sense organs and motor organs along with the mind.

Shadripus: Six enemies hinder spiritual progress and destroy morality:

1. Kama (Desires): is the starter of chain reaction.
2. Krodha (Anger): Desires grow by fulfilling them. When they are interrupted, this causes anger.
3. Lobha (Greed): Desires grow in the form of greed. One wants to accumulate.
4. Mada (Ego): Desire wants one to exhibit prowess and control others.
5. Moha (Attachment): One wants to hold onto possessions.

6. Matsar (Jealousy): One becomes a rival and wants to beat the competitor.

Short-sighted vs. visionary: If you are short-sighted, you will respond to your senses and the mind. You will be blind. You will react to the impulses for which you may regret. If you are a visionary, you will have a panoramic view of life. You will act constructively.

Silence (Mauna): Silence has inner strength and talks louder than speech, action or body language. Mauna preserves energy. One should restrain two sense organs and one motor organ. See no evil, hear no evil and say no evil.

Skillful action: Skillful action is called Karma yoga. Skillful action is efficient because it is done with love and without expectation of results or related stress. Actions done selflessly as an instrument do not produce any sanskaras.

Surrender: Surrender means attunement. Tune your energy to the energy of the universe. Fighting with universal energy will result in stress and failure. By surrendering to the image of a deity, you attract divine qualities to your life.

Transformation-conversion: Transformation gives you the power to choose. You become rooted as the master of Self. Conversion makes you a slave to others. Masses of people are blind followers. Converting to a cause or religion is an escape and relief for them.

Unity of life: Realize that we are interconnected with nature and the entire creation. Live and flow in rhythm with nature. Remain compassionate toward all living creatures.

Vidya (Wisdom): Wisdom provides liberation. Other knowledge earns wealth. Information and social status. Information, knowledge, and logic are only means, yet they can trap you. Wisdom guides you to transform your life. Wisdom comes from a pure, receptive mind, intention and awareness.

Virtues (Niyamas): Cultivate five virtues. These support meditation.

1. Shauch (purity of body and mind)
2. Tapas (austerities) are used to burn impurities.
3. Santosh (contentment)
4. Swadhaya (study of Self)
5. Ishwar pranidhana (surrender to the Supreme)

Vivek (Spiritual discernment): Vivek is the ability to discriminate between permanent and impermanent. Vivek produces renunciation effortlessly.

Vairagya (Renunciation): After one experiences Vivek, wrong attachments drop away like dry leaves.

Yamas (Restraints): These sustain Dharma.

1. Ahinsa (Non-violence)
2. Satya (Truth)
3. Asteya (Non-stealing_
4. Brahmacharya (Celibacy)
5. Aparigraha (Non-greediness)

About the Author

Yogi Shanti Desai with his family in 2021

Yogi Shanti Desai is a revolutionary thinker and yoga master. He has studied ancient scriptures subjectively, extracted their essence, and written extensively on his findings in twenty-one previous books. Yogi Shanti recommends students to be self-reliant and not follow teachings blindly. His simplified philosophy is applicable to the layperson.

Publications

Yoga: Holistic Practice Manual	1976
Hatha Yoga Practice Manual	1978
Meditation Practice Manual	1981
Reality Here and Now	1996
Self- I, Me, Mine, Ours, Illusions	2002
Dynamic Balanced Living	2004
Dynamic Meditation for Living	2006
Dynamic Quantum Transformation	2007
Personal to Global Transformation	2007
Wisdom for Living	2009
The Secret of Bliss	2011
Dynamic Spiritual Transformation	2012
Zero is Infinity	2015
Wake Up	2017
Quantum Leap to Liberation	2017
Spiritual Awakening in the Age of Kali Yuga	2018
Threefold Path to Bliss	2018
Transformation of Consciousness	2020
Eternal Reality	2020
Recognizing Blessings in Disguise	2020
Ancient Wisdom for Transforming the Present Age	2021
Applying the Essential Wisdom of Vedanta to Everyday Life	2022

www.yogishantidesai.com